ALL THINGS NEW

stories of
transformed lives

What Others Are Saying About 'All Things New'

Matt's book is essentially stories of hope and all things renewed. Real life faith is a struggle, it's sweaty and hard work and these stories reflect that. It's refreshing to read about the tension our faith holds with the active good news and the now and not yet. All things are indeed New in Christ and I encourage you to read these stories of that truth. Lives are changed when they meet Jesus.

Cris Rogers *(Author, Rector of All Hallows Bow, UK)*

One of the most relevant and powerful things we can share with others is our testimony. Our story of how we have encountered Jesus and the difference He has made in our lives. Like the Bible says in Revelation 12:11 we overcome our enemy by the word of our testimony. In this book we read about ordinary people like you and me who have encountered Jesus and have overcome our adversary.

I would like to express my gratitude to Matt McChlery for compiling these inspiring and encouraging stories. My prayer is that you would be impacted by them and encouraged to tell others what Jesus has done for you.

Rob McFarlane *(Pastor of River Church, UK)*

This collection of personal stories will encourage your heart and stir up your faith. Thanks Matt for telling us your story and the stories of others too. Like Matt, I also began a relationship with Jesus when I was thirteen. And since then He has turned my world upside down, taking me from the banks of the Zambezi to the bustle of Berlin. And now it's your turn. Jesus can make all things new in your life too!

Gareth Lowe *(Pastor of Every Nation Church - Berlin, Germany)*

Matt is a very gifted musician and worship leader and I've been blessed in the past through his ministry. Having this book I can now say I've been blessed afresh by the stories Matt brings and the insights about the Lord and his Kingdom they contain.

Tony Cummings *(Music Editor - Cross Rhythms Radio, UK)*

ALL THINGS NEW

stories of
transformed lives

Matt McChlery

FAITHSEED
BOOKS

First Published © Matt McChlery 2017. This Second Edition Published in 2021 by Faithseed Books (an imprint of Matt McChlery Ministries), 34 Windsor Drive, Wisbech, PE13 3HJ, United Kingdom.

ISBN: 978-1-7398024-1-7

Cover design © Ryan Baker-Barnes.

~

For my darling wife

Verity

I am yours forever!

~

Contents

Foreword 11

Introduction 13

1. Freedom's Story 17
2. My Story 29
3. Fiona's Story 39
4. Bob's Story 47
5. Simon's Story 53
6. Sally's Story 59
7. Terry's Story 63
8. Verity's Story 69
9. What's Your Story? 73

Thanks 93

About The Author 95

Foreword

I am privileged to be able to add my words to all that Matt has compiled here. I knew well the land of Matt's birth, Zimbabwe, and all of the individuals whose moving stories are included here. For 10 years my wife, Robyn, and I shared intimately in the lives of each of them as part of the same church fellowship. So I can attest to the truth of all that Matt shares of himself and of these precious disciples of the Lord Jesus Christ.

We live in a world where society has sought to marginalise religion and silence all who have found freedom in Christ. What a tragedy! Under the façade that many put up in public are similar struggles with lives broken by their own sin and those who sin against them, dashed hopes, mental and physical suffering, addictions. Yet the stories of all shared in this book show that there is a way out from the darkness and despair that afflicts so many.

Matt has produced this beautiful little book which I trust will help many to also find freedom, peace, joy and hope for the future.

Patrick Johnstone
Author Emeritus of Operation World

Introduction

Sitting down to think about the concept of a new CD can take many months, indeed years. And this has been the case with the process that has gone on behind the scenes to put together the 6-track worship EP 'All Things New'. Having finally settled on the general theme of the recording: 'Salvation', it was then a matter of selecting the various songs. The process of weeding out those that were too weak lyrically or did not sit sonically alongside the others. Then the re-writing process needed to be done where certain elements of the chosen songs needed to be improved upon in order to make them work better as well as to help them to be used within a congregational setting.

In amongst all the thinking, planning, re-writing and recording it occurred to me that an important element of the project was missing. We had written and recorded some amazing songs for people to sing to help them express their worship of God. We had songs that talked about salvation, about what Jesus had done for us. But it would mean nothing if people did not know what salvation *is*. And if people *did* know what salvation is, our worship is all the more sweeter and meaningful if we remind each other and ourselves of how God has worked in our lives. How He has and continues to change us day by day. Not simply knocking off some of the rough edges and re-painting over the cracks. No! But completely re-creating us. This led to the writing of this book. It has taken a lot longer than I originally intended – several years longer – but it is finally done and ready to be read by you.

This book aims to do two things. Firstly, it will explain why we need God's glorious and most generous gift of salvation and what salvation is. Secondly, it will fill our spirits with awe, wonder and thanksgiving as we read about how others' lives have been made new as they have accepted God's free and precious gift of freedom and new life.

As you read this book, I hope and pray that you will receive a fresh touch of God's Spirit; that you will be encouraged and inspired to lift your voice in worship to The One who has indeed made all things new!

Matt McChlery

CHAPTER ONE

Freedom's Story

L et me tell you a story about ancient things established at the dawn of time that are embedded deep within the foundations of creation. A story about betrayal and a love stronger than death. Let me tell you a story where freedom is not only a concept or a state of being, but where Freedom is a person! This is a story that has turned the world upside down and continues to change the lives of people that hear it and believe it, because Freedom's story is true.

This is a story we all desperately need to hear, for the truth is humanity lives under a curse. This curse separates us from God. This curse has defiled God's creation. We live in a world that is not as it should be. Humanity is a broken reflection of what God intended when He created us, when He breathed life into those fists of clay:

'GOD formed Man out of dirt from the ground and blew into his nostrils the breath of life. The Man came alive — a living soul!'

(Genesis 2:7, The Message)

Paradise Lost

After God had created the world, He made mankind in His own image[1]. God gave the first people, Adam and Eve, a beautiful place where they could live in harmony with nature, each other and with God. It was a paradise and was called Eden. He told Adam that he could eat from any tree in that place except for one, the tree of the knowledge of good and evil[2]. If anyone did eat from

---

[1] Genesis 1:26
[2] Genesis 2:17

it, they would die. By this time, death had not entered the world as creation was still as God had intended, pure and perfect. However, this did not last long.

One day, while Eve was out and about, a devil-possessed serpent tempted her to eat from the forbidden tree. Eve tried to resist but eventually gave in to the temptation and ate its fruit. She then gave some to Adam and he ate it too[3]. As soon as this act of disobedience towards God had happened, sin entered the world and humankind's relationship with God was forever altered. A supernatural law became established and entwined within the destiny of all humanity.

Adam and Eve certainly gained the knowledge of good and evil. They suddenly realised they were no longer pure. They recognised the evil within them that had come about by their act of disobedience. Knowing they had sinned against God, they were ashamed and understood that their relationship with God was changed forever. So later when they heard God walking in the garden they ran and hid from him[4].

---

[3] Genesis 3:1-7
[4] Genesis 3:8-10

Adam and Eve's disobedience incurred punishment. As God had warned them, the consequence for their sin was death:

> 'Cursed is the ground because of you;
> through painful toil you will eat food from it
> all the days of your life.
> It will produce thorns and thistles for you,
> and you will eat the plants of the field.
> By the sweat of your brow
> you will eat your food
> until you return to the ground,
> since from it you were taken;
> for dust you are
> and to dust you will return.'

(Genesis 3: 17-19, NIV)

Eventually they would die, and so would every human being after them.

Humanity's relationship with God was forever altered. Adam and Eve were cast out of Eden and out of God's presence[5]. From now on, for any sin-filled human to enter into the presence of God, they had to do so through the shedding of blood. A life had to be given in sacrifice as a payment for their sin. God established this

---

[5] Genesis 3:23-24

when he killed an animal and made clothes for Adam and Eve[6]. Indeed we can see this law being kept throughout the Old Testament where the Israelites offered sacrifices to God.

Although Paradise had been lost along with humanity's relationship with God a glimmer of hope still remained. Even in the very beginning, God had a plan to rescue mankind from sin. Freedom's story had begun and was woven into God's master plan to make all things new once more.

As God cursed the serpent for his part in Adam and Eve's betrayal, He foretells of a son of Eve who will come and crush Satan (symbolised by the serpent) and break this curse by sacrificing his life:

> 'I will put enmity
> between you and the woman,
> and between your offspring and hers;
> he will crush your head,
> and you will strike his heel.'

(Genesis 3:15, NIV)

---

[6] Genesis 3:21

The Saviour Comes

Many years later, God's rescue plan swings into action in a small town called Bethlehem. A young couple, Joseph and Mary had travelled from their home town of Nazareth to the place where Joseph's family came from in order to be counted in a census that was taking place throughout the Roman world[7]. Both Mary and Joseph had been visited by an angel on separate occasions who told them that Mary, who was a virgin[8], would conceive miraculously by The Holy Spirit and give birth to a son[9]. They were told to call him Jesus.

It was important that Mary was a virgin when she conceived for multiple reasons. Firstly, God himself needed to be the father of His son. Having a mortal seed substitute the supernatural power of God simply would not work. Secondly, the curse of original sin that was placed upon mankind when Adam and Eve fell is passed down from generation to generation. As conception occurs and a new life is created the curse of sin and separation from God is passed on[10]. Mary being a virgin when she conceived, and

---

[7] Luke 2:1-5
[8] Luke 1:34
[9] Luke 1:35
[10] Romans 5:12

conceiving by the power of the Holy Spirit means that the chain of original sin is broken which means Jesus can live a perfect and sinless life[11].

Unfortunately this vitally important event has over time become romanticised and commercialised. It is often quite difficult to separate the glitter and tinsel from the reality of the historic event we are remembering. Even some of the carols we sing do not accurately portray the biblical account of the birth of Jesus.

Jesus' birth was like any other. It was messy. It was painful. He was born into poverty amongst the animals. It was not glamorous. It did not give anyone that 'Christmassy feeling'. God became man and entered the world just like any other human being does. Jesus behaved just like any other baby does, complete with crying and bodily functions. Yet this was still a miracle; the divine becoming flesh. Freedom had come!

Jesus was, and still is, God's rescue plan. The gifts He was given at His birth by the Magi symbolised who He was and the destiny He was to fulfil[12]. The gift of gold indicated   Jesus' supernatural kingship and majesty. Frankincense, a type of

---

[11] Isaiah 53:9, I Peter 2:22
[12] Matthew 2:11

incense, symbolised His priestly role. Myrrh was an ingredient used in the embalming of bodies and foretells Jesus' destiny and the fulfilment of God's rescue plan.

Perfect Sacrifice

Jesus lived a fully human life. He gave people a clearer and better understanding of God. He was tempted but He did not sin[13]. All through His life, Jesus moved closer towards his ultimate destiny, of becoming Freedom for us; the way by which all of humanity could be rescued from sin and set free from its chains. But the law of God that was established at the foundation of the world demands the shedding of blood to make us clean, to take away our sin in order for us to be able to enter His presence. A life needs to be given. Something, or indeed someone, needs to die!

Now traditional animal sacrifices required an animal that was perfect, without deformity or discolouration of its coat[14]. Jesus, being free from the curse of sin and living a life that was without sin qualified Him and Him alone to become the ultimate sacrifice,

---

[13] Hebrews 4:15
[14] Leviticus 22:19-25

the ultimate payment for the sin of the world[15]. When Jesus died on the cross, He became sin on our behalf. He broke the curse and bridged the gap that had separated man from God for so long:

> God made him who had no sin to be sin for us, so that in him we might become the righteousness of God.
>
> (2 Corinthians 5:21, NIV)

Jesus became our eternal and final sacrifice. By placing sin upon a sinless sacrifice, upon a divine sacrifice, the power of sin and death were broken. The curse placed upon humanity at the time of Adam and Eve is forever broken! Humanity now has access to God once more. We are no longer separated from His presence because Jesus has paid our ultimate punishment for sin with His death. Jesus is Freedom. It is only through Jesus that we can be set free from the power of sin and be reconnected with God[16].

---

[15] Romans 8:3
[16] John 14:6

Ultimate Victory

But wait. Freedom's story does not end with Jesus dying on the cross. No, there is more. God's freedom plan is not yet complete.

Jesus was dead. He was buried in a tomb. But three days later when some of his followers came to anoint His body with embalming oils, Jesus was not there!

> At the crack of dawn on Sunday, the women came to the tomb carrying the burial spices they had prepared. They found the entrance stone rolled back from the tomb, so they walked in. But once inside, they couldn't find the body of the Master Jesus.
>
> (Luke 24:1-3, The Message)

Remember, Jesus was fully human but he was also fully God. The divine made flesh. The punishment for sin is separation from God and death. But Jesus changed all this because He supernaturally rose again!

> 'Why are you looking for the Living One in a cemetery? He is not here, but raised up. Remember how he told you when you were still back in Galilee that he had to be handed over to sinners, be killed on a cross, and in three days rise up?' Then they remembered Jesus' words.

(Luke 24:5-8, The Message)

Jesus conquered the power of sin by dying, and He defeated the power of death by rising again. The curse is now completely broken. Freedom came to set us free not just for this life, but for eternity.

CHAPTER TWO

My Story

I was born and raised in Zimbabwe, Africa. My parents were both teachers and we lived on the school campus of whichever school my parents were teaching at. I lived in Zimbabwe's capital city, Harare, until I was eight-years-old. I vaguely remember attending the Sunday School at the nearby Presbyterian church and singing some of the typical Sunday School songs that you often can still hear in school assemblies today. I'm sure we also did some art and craft activities, but I can't remember with any sort of accuracy. The point is, I had some knowledge about God and Jesus but it was very external. Yes, someone called Jesus used to exist and I knew Christmas was Jesus' birthday party. I knew you went to church to learn about Jesus. But it had no immediate relevance to my life at this point.

When I was roughly eight-years-old my father was given an amazing job opportunity. He was asked to move out into the middle of a farming area an hour's drive to the north of the capital city and to be the founding headmaster of a new school that was about to be built there. I still remember our first journey there. We piled into the blue Renault 4 family car which had the gear stick coming horizontally out of the centre of the dashboard. Provisions of sandwiches, drinks, sweets to eat on the journey, wet flannels (just in case – of what I don't know) and in-the-car games at the ready. We seldom travelled far by car in those days.

We had been travelling for about an hour. The city was far behind us. Acres and acres of farmland stretched out either side of the road, occasionally interrupted by mud huts or areas of virgin African bushveld. We pulled up opposite a road-side bottle store and stopped. Apart from the store, there was nothing else nearby. We headed off into the bush, the elephant grass was taller than me. After a little while of what we called 'bundu-bashing' we stopped and Dad announced that we were now standing where our new house was going to be! It was hard for me to imagine that a house and indeed an entire school would soon be built and dramatically transform this area of unused land forever.

Soon after that the building began and we moved there. I continued my primary education at Barwick School, the new school my father founded. The nearest shop was miles and miles away! We travelled back to Harare about once or twice a week to stock up on provisions which completely loaded up the car's boot. We were literally in the middle of nowhere, living 'in the sticks' as Zimbabwean's describe it. There was no church nearby, so we did not go. We did sing Christian songs at school assemblies and said prayers. But it was still a case of an external head-knowledge of this Jesus person who used to exist but didn't mean much to me really.

Sooner that I thought my time at primary school came to an end and I was fortunate enough to be given a place at one of the most prominent senior schools in the country; Peterhouse.

It was a completely new world! I had attended boarding schools at primary level, but only as a day pupil. Now I was a resident living apart from my parents for three weeks at a time ninety miles away. I suddenly had decisions to make that would affect who I would grow up to become.

I started off trying to take the path of least resistance. I joined in with the swearing and bad language of the other boys, more as a way of trying to fit in and be accepted than any other reason. I had already come to the decision that I did not want to smoke, so that temptation was easier to avoid and I was prepared to be stronger and refuse it if ever it came to it. I got into a few fights with one particular boy in my year group who I did not see eye to eye with at all. I was trying to fit in, trying to be one of the lads. But to be honest this always left me with an uneasy feeling as it was not really who I was or who I wanted to be deep inside.

I had discovered singing at primary school and I knew I enjoyed it. Peterhouse is an Anglican (Church of England) school and its chapel choir had (and still has) a very good reputation. I made it my goal to join the choir. So at the first opportunity I went along to the auditions and was so pleased when I was selected to join. I was given my choir robes and really felt special as we processed in down the aisle and took our places in the choir stalls at the very front of the chapel every Sunday.

It was great being in the choir! You got to miss rest time after lunch almost every day in order to attend rehearsals; you had to leave homework early when you had to prepare for a church service; you were allowed to walk on a certain patch of lawn in front of the music rooms because of your choir membership; you got to attend social functions as well as travel to other schools and even a conference or two in order to perform.

We sung traditional hymns that are centuries old. One thing I do remember quite clearly is how the words within these ancient songs began to have an effect on me. As I was exposed to them for extended periods of time I began to think about what the words were saying. Something began to stir within me although at the time I did not know what. I began to ask myself questions about God and Jesus as I tried to understand what these hymns were getting at. This was more of a subconscious musing rather than an overt seeking for God, but something was happening inside me at that time.

About one term into my first year of senior school the boy who slept opposite me, George, asked me if I wanted to go with him to a Christian thing that happened on a Thursday evening during the second half of homework time. I thought this was brilliant – homework was no fun! So I went along.

Well, it was the strangest and weirdest thing I had ever experienced and was completely not what I was expecting, although come to think of it I don't know quite what I was expecting, but it wasn't that! One of the teachers had a guitar and there was an overhead projector shining the words to the songs onto the wall. There was quite a crowd of pupils of all ages there and they were all singing with great enthusiasm. I found it very peculiar that they were clapping along to the songs and lifting up their hands – this did not happen in the choir! I had never experienced faith being expressed in this way before and it did feel a bit strange. I was unsure if I would go back again.

But somehow the next few Thursday evenings I found myself going back again and again and over time I began to know some of the songs so joined in. I also had a go at clapping along. It was quite fun actually and definitely better than homework! Over the next few weeks and months I was really enjoying attending this group they called 'Christian Forum'. The talks were inspiring and were starting to answer some of these questions that the hymns had been stirring up. I was also finding that I was freer to be who I was in the company of these people rather than trying to pretend to be something that I wasn't. As a result I started to develop some good friendships, the strongest one being with George.

Around half way through my first year, in the wintery rugby season, there was a special event. Little did I know that this event was to change my life forever! Some old-boys from the school who had gone to university in Cape Town had formed a band with some others they had met there called 'Penguins in Africa'. They had done some touring around South Africa and were in Zimbabwe so they were invited to give a concert for the whole school on a Saturday evening.

It was amazing! It was all outdoors. The school chapel was the background of the stage. There were a series of steps leading down from the walkway in front of the chapel. At the base of the steps was a large open area of walkways and lawns that spread out in front of the chapel. All the pupils stood in the open area at the base of the stairs. I seem to remember they might have also brought in some of the rugby stands to put at the back of the audience area for those at the back to use. The staff somehow managed to get onto a flat part of the dining hall roof which was to the side of the audience area and had even managed to get a few sofas up there. There was a big sound system and some lighting. The band took to the stage and it began!

The lead singer appeared in a spotlight on the roof of the chapel! He sung the opening number from up there then came down to the stage to join the rest of the band. They sung upbeat songs about Jesus, God, sin and salvation. I could feel my insides just wanting to burst. Something was going on – something big –

something amazing! Everything I had been thinking about started to make sense. The reason why the people at Christian Forum sung so vigorously and clapped their hands started to make sense. Something inside me was just saying 'Yes!' Then a point in the concert was reached where they stopped singing and the lead singer took a few moments to explain that we were all sinners and had fallen short of God's plan for us. We were guilty and separated from God. He explained that Jesus died to take our sins away and that we could come back to God if we asked Jesus into our hearts and lives. He then asked those who wanted to make a commitment to Jesus to raise their hands. Hands went up everywhere – mine went up too. We then prayed a prayer together. I prayed that prayer with tears rolling down my cheeks. Something happened to me that night. Jesus knocked on the door of my heart and I let Him in. I had just turned thirteen and my new life was just beginning. I have never been the same again since.

Since that day my life has been a faith-filled amazing journey of growth and self-discovery. I have seen God work in people's lives in miraculous ways as well as experiencing God's presence in the ordinary. I have grown, changed, been to university, relocated half way around the world, married the love of my life and experienced the joy of the birth of our two children. There is so much I could say about what Jesus means to me and how He has been continually at work in my life, changing and transforming me it would be far too long to contain in a neat chapter. I would need a whole book!

God is full of grace and compassion. He does deal with the things in our lives that are not right, but does so lovingly. He also does so gradually. You are not suddenly confronted with all the sin in your life all in one go. God will begin dealing with things a couple at a time. Then when one thing is sorted, He will move on to the next. It is all part of the journey of becoming more like Christ. As we walk with Him, obey Him and live to please Him, He changes us.

However, I don't want to mislead you. The Christian life can be a hard one. It is not an easy 'get out of jail free' card. Yes, my life is full of purpose and joy but bad things still happen. Jesus does not wrap us up in cotton wool and protect us from the dangers and pain of the world.

In 2016 I was unexpectedly diagnosed with non-Hodgkin's Lymphoma, cancer of the lymphatic system. This was a time of great pain, sadness and suffering. Yet it was also a time of great joy and knowing the real presence of God. When faced with death you really find out what you appreciate about life. One thing I know for certain is that without my faith in Jesus I would have crumbled under the pressure of my circumstances. I would not have coped. I have learned that it is by going through the pain, by walking with Jesus through the hard times, this is when we get to know Him more. This is when we grow! In late 2016 I was given the all-clear and am now in full remission.

I now rest in the fact that I know God is in control. Nobody is beyond his ability to save, or change, or heal. My life is in His hands. Every day is a gift for me to use for His glory, to make the world a better place and to point people towards Him.

CHAPTER THREE

Fiona's Story

Fiona was under the care of the Mental Health Services for many years. Ever since the birth of her children she was in and out of hospital with a whole range of mental health problems. She always felt she was a terrible mother, that the responsibility now placed upon her was too great.

With the stresses and strains of motherhood taking their toll combined with post-natal depression, one day Fiona found herself fighting thoughts of throwing her precious new baby into a river. It was at this point she decided she was a bad person.

Things did not improve with the birth of her second child. Another bout of the 'baby blues' took hold. Fiona believed everyone was out to get her. She just wanted to end it all and was going to burn down the house in a desperate attempt to escape, by taking her own life.

Over the years, Fiona has been diagnosed with an extremely wide variety of mental health illnesses including: bi-polar disorder, psychotic depression and unstable emotional personality just to name a few. She has been admitted to hospital on a number of occasions and has undergone thirty lots of Electro Convulsive Therapy (ECT).

Her life eventually began to improve after the ECT but things were still very unstable. When she was having a good moment, Fiona felt empty and disconnected from the world, like she was just going through the motions. Often feeling like she was simply a cardboard cut-out, simply existing. These feelings often led to self-harming and then a spiral back down into the depths of despair and depression.

Life carried on like this for several years until Fiona experienced a very dark time in 2008.

Fiona had just been through a long period of time when sleep was extremely poor. During these moments of anxiety and sleeplessness, she would often drive her car about late at night in an attempt to calm herself or to take her mind off her fears. However, it was during this time when the body of a man was found beside the main road near to where she lived. Fiona was convinced that she was responsible for his death. It was obvious to her that whilst driving about in the depths of the night, she had knocked him down with her car. It reached a point where she was so convinced she was responsible that she was even having images of the man's face and the clothes he was wearing. Also during this time a series of arson attacks were happening in the nearby town. These were being reported on the TV news and Fiona was convinced she was also responsible for these as well as other injustices or disasters that were reported.

Fiona's life of fear and extreme stress continued to intensify. She was convinced the police would soon be knocking on her door and was afraid that the secret of her 'crimes' would be discovered. She felt completely unworthy of love and saw herself as evil. At this time she was cutting herself frequently and required stitches on twenty occasions in one month. Certain that she would lose her family if the 'truth' came out, she was in anguish thinking that she was hurting them. All she wanted to do was to escape. To feel a release of all the shame, guilt and condemnation that was bubbling inside. Surely her family would be better off without her?

So late that night, she got a bowl and some very powerful prescription medication. She removed the pills from their blister packs and had them all loose and rattling about in the bowl. In her distress, Fiona swallowed more than several lethal doses, taking three or four at a time. She was already hysterical, but taking the overdose made her even more so. Driving sometimes helped to clear her head, so she got in the car and drove. Somewhere in her mind she was thinking, 'Where would I die?', 'Who would find me?', 'What would my family really feel?'.

She drove to an empty car park in the nearby town and reached out for help. She phoned the Samaritans, a twenty-four hour helpline. Between her sobs she told the woman on the other end of the phone what she had done. The woman's voice was calm and reassuring, like that of an angel. She listened to Fiona's problems for around twenty minutes or so and then suggested that perhaps Fiona would be better off calling an ambulance so that she could die in a hospital rather than in a car park. So Fiona called an ambulance.

After being rushed to hospital, Fiona was overcome with sickness. It felt as if her stomach had been turned inside out. She was admitted and taken to a ward where she cried and cried for hours.

The following night when the ward was quiet, she was overcome with fear. She began to think about life after death and what that would be like for her. She was afraid to go to sleep in case she died and the devil would get her. So she prayed. She prayed to the one and only God she believed was real, the God who created Heaven and Earth. She prayed for forgiveness. Being truly sorry she wanted to escape from the inevitability of her situation, although she did not believe there was much hope of that. The pills were extremely strong and lesser doses had proved fatal.

It was then that Fiona heard a voice. It was a strong, clear audible voice that spoke with strength and authority. Fiona knew it was the voice of God. He spoke and told her that she would be alright and that she should go and lead a life of worship.

Looking around the room it was clear that nobody else had heard this voice. Most of the patients were asleep and the nurses were at their station. She had no idea how to lead a life of worship, but she promised she would go to church and find out how to do so.

An internet search led her to a friendly evangelical church that was located in the nearby town. Being slightly apprehensive of what people might think when they discovered her reason for coming to the church, Fiona summoned up the courage and went. When she arrived she was amazed to discover that she was accepted as she was. She could feel the presence of God in that place. During a time of prayer, a lady called Anna prayed with her. After asking God for strength and peace for Fiona, Anna told her that she was a child of God and that she was forgiven because of Jesus.

The following week, Fiona went back to the same church. The message was about a passage in Mark 5 where Jesus heals a demon-possessed man. To Fiona it felt as though the sermon was just for her. This Bible story echoed so much of her life it was obvious that God was speaking to her. This demon-possessed man lived among the tombs, cut himself with rocks and could not be restrained, even with chains. Jesus commanded the evil spirits to leave the man and sent them into a nearby heard of pigs, all of which rushed down a steep bank into a lake and were all drowned.

Fiona knew this was her story. Jesus had already saved her from death. The doctor in the hospital was amazed that she has survived. God had spoken directly to her with an audible voice and Jesus was now making His presence known in her life as the living God.

Since meeting Jesus and giving her life to Him, Fiona's life has improved vastly. She will be the first to tell you that she is not completely healed of her depression and mental health issues, but the intensity of them is much reduced and bad days happen less frequently. It is like someone has turned the volume down. She still needs to take medication, but is walking through her healing with God, step by step, day by day.

When she prays at night a deep sense of peace and calm washes over her and settles her mind. She is eager to learn more of God and is fully committed to living a life of worship that she promised she would. Fiona has been baptized and she continues to move closer to Jesus being transformed from the person she was into the person God has created her to be. Fiona has found a continuing joy that she receives through small improvements in her life, knowing that God loves her and has forgiven her.

There are times when things still go wrong in Fiona's life but this Bible passage gives her hope and reassurance:

For if the great apostle Paul still had issues that kept resurfacing in his life, it is ok if the same happens to us. However, just as Paul was continually moving towards God, we should be too. Sin is not an excuse, but it is helpful to know that others struggle just as you do. When Fiona slips God lifts her and steers her onto a better path.

With this new found freedom she has received from God, Fiona has got more involved in the local church as well as volunteering at a nearby maximum security prison where she serves tea and looks after visiting children in the visitor's hall.

> "For I do not do the good I want to do, but the evil I do not want to do—this I keep on doing. Now if I do what I do not want to do, it is no longer I who do it, but it is sin living in me that does it."
>
> (Romans 7:19-20)

It is amazing to see God at work in Fiona's life, rebuilding the broken and restoring the shattered places. It is also fantastic to see Fiona allowing God to work in her life. I will conclude her story with her own words: "No one said life in this world would be easy, but God's grace means I can survive the journey until I am with Him for eternity"

CHAPTER FOUR

Bob's Story

Before Bob became a Christian he had a sense that God existed but his faith never went beyond that. Starting off in a very traditional church that he found boring, repetitive and irrelevant, faith was something aloof and removed from his life. Churchgoing mainly consisted of going to weddings and funerals.

Bob's life was also extremely busy with his career taking up the majority of his time and attention. Bob worked as a bus conductor which took up eighty hours a week. He then worked for the police as a Special Constable which involved lots of events. It was during this time that he was also involved with the Scouts organisation and this involved going to church once in a while. These tended to be less formal occasions and Bob found them more relaxed and comfortable. He also worked as a fire fighter and worked on oil rigs, all of which took up a lot of time and prevented Bob from exploring church and a relationship with Jesus further.

Bob loves working with people and enjoyed his work very much. What he did, helping others, made him feel fulfilled even though it took up almost all of his time. Nevertheless, the job was very stressful and there was a time when Bob went through some difficulties at work which lead to him becoming very angry. Bob felt an emptiness inside but circumstances prevented him from going to church to see if this is where he would find fulfilment.

Later in life, Bob retired due to ill health and he and his family relocated to a new part of the country. This is when he met David.

David lived next door and Bob struck up a friendship with him and his wife, Sally. Both Bob and David had time on their hands and as their friendship grew, David came around and they talked for ages about things they enjoyed and books they had read. As time went on, the discussion moved on to the Bible but conversation remained easy, flowing and non-judgemental. Bob found he was learning things from David all the time.

After not seeing David for a while Bob learned that David had sadly died of a terminal illness. So David got in touch with Sally. It was during this conversation that Sally mentioned that she and David went to a church in town which she invited him to.

Seeing something fresh in David's life and having talked to him about what he believed and why, Bob was curious to go to the church where David went. When he got there it was a completely different experience of church to what he had encountered before. The first thing Bob noticed was how happy the people were who went there. The Bible teaching applied to modern life and addressed things he was struggling with as well as teaching him more about Jesus. There was lively music lead by a band. Bob is a fan of electric guitars and live music, so he really made a deep connection with the music and songs. He found that church could be enjoyable and relevant and he enjoyed going along.

After a while, Bob joined a few of the church groups where he was able to learn more about God. As he did this, he realised that he needed to make a decision whether he too would follow Jesus or not. So he prayed and asked God to lead him. What developed was a strong desire to be baptised.

Bob felt that the time was right, to make a decision to follow Jesus and to be baptised. The church leaders agreed to baptise Bob, but he was unsure of an exact date when this would happen. So, Bob took a step of faith and packed a small blue sports bag which included a change of clothes and a towel. He took this bag to church with him every week, just in case he would get baptised then.

Bob did not have to wait too long. The baptismal pool was soon hired and Bob, along with a couple of others were baptised. Bob gave his testimony and committed his life to Jesus. He remembers it as an awesome day full of excitement; a day when he felt the presence of God so strongly in his life.

Bob has suffered from PTSD (Post Traumatic Stress Disorder) for many years. A while after his baptism he began having some very distressing nightmares where a particularly traumatic event he had experienced in his life kept playing over and over in his mind. The dreams were very distressing and felt very real. Bob was also suffering from feelings of guilt and was fighting urges to harm himself. It was at a men's group meeting during this time when he broke down and asked the others in the group to pray for him. So they did. They prayed and anointed Bob with oil. He felt a strong presence of the Holy Spirit and his whole body went warm. At the same time a wave of calm washed over him. From this point on, Bob enjoyed many months of peaceful sleep. The horror had gone from his dreams.

Bob has learnt that he can always speak to God; that He doesn't forget you. This has helped to make him more relaxed and calm. He feels he has also got a lot better at prayer. Having never prayed before, now after giving it a go for a while it comes more easily and he is growing in confidence with it.

CHAPTER FIVE

Simon's Story

One of four children, with an alcoholic father who drank away much of the wages he brought home, Simon's start in life was not ideal. Playing the class clown at school in order to compensate for underachievement, Simon was eventually suspended and left school with just one O-Level in English.

When Simon was sixteen, his father kicked him out of the house after Simon confronted him. This sent him into a spiral of violence, drugs and theft. He also became a demonstrator and regularly got into trouble for public offences as he was involved with a group that demonstrated regularly and pushed the limits. By this time drugs had become a big part of Simon's life and would continue to dominate most of his life for the next twenty nine years.

Despite having a drug problem, Simon managed to find and keep work which included work in warehouses as well as working overseas for several years as a stevedore. At one point, Simon worked as a debt collector for a drug dealer. As a seven foot tall man, he was intimidating and hard to forget!

Throughout this time, Simon's thieving knew no limits. He was an opportunist and even family and friends were not immune from becoming a victim.

By the time he was forty five, Simon was married with a wife and three kids. However, his marriage only lasted eight years because he did not put into it what he should have and was still drinking and taking drugs. He had a job as a manager and managed to maintain this on weekdays whilst living wildly on the weekends, feeding a heavy cocaine habit. He was literally leading a double life; his work colleagues had no idea.

Then it all fell apart!

Simon's ex-wife and children were living next to a particularly bad neighbour. This neighbour would bully and harass Simon's family, at one time hospitalising his ex-wife after attacking her as well as regularly bullying and beating up his son.

This went on for several years, then things had seemed to have calmed down for about six months or so. Simon was relieved that it had stopped.

One Saturday evening Simon was in the pub and had been drinking heavily and taking cocaine. He received a call from his ex-wife who was distressed and told Simon that this neighbour had broken their son's nose and cut his arm with a bottle.

Simon had had enough. This was the end. This had to stop! Simon saw red. He armed himself with a samurai sword and a bayonet and kicked down the door of the neighbour. The person he was looking for was not there, although his parents were. So he terrorised them for a while before storming out and continuing his search by going on a rampage through three more houses. Throughout the whole episode, Simon felt detached from what he was doing and said it felt like an out of body experience.

The next day, Simon saw the man he was after. He knocked him out and then handed himself in to the nearest police station. He was fairly convinced that he would get away with it especially once he had told the police about the other circumstances. However, he did not. He was sent to prison for two, one year sentences, to be served consecutively.

A few months into his sentence, Simon was moved to a different prison called Spring Hill, which is an open prison. It was here where Simon was introduced to the Prison Fellowship.

Simon is a coffee enthusiast. The only coffee available to him at Spring Hill was the instant variety, which he did not approve of at all. It was during a discussion with a fellow inmate about the woes of not having access to good coffee when the inmate suggested that if he went along to a Prison Fellowship meeting, he would be able to get some good filter coffee there.

Simon had nothing against people of faith, in fact he admired them. He enjoyed the worship at the first meeting and decided to keep going. He enjoyed learning about the Bible, the history and singing songs. It was here that he realised that he was at his lowest point and really needed God.

At night all he could think about was Jesus and what He had done for him. Simon felt God was saying to him, "Commit to me or walk away". So Simon chose to commit. The way in which he wanted to mark this decision was to get baptised. So he spoke to the prison chaplain. The baptism was extremely difficult to organise and he was told at every turn that it could not happen.

So, Simon had a meeting with the deputy prison warden. He left the meeting finally with the 'yes' he was hoping for, allowing the baptism to go ahead. It was only later that Simon learned that the deputy warden had intended to say no.

The baptism was a wonderful occasion for Simon. Volunteers from the Prison Fellowship were there and Simon was encouraged that his story of transformation could be a pillar of hope for other offenders.

Whilst still in prison, Simon also took part in the Sycamore Tree course run by the Prison Fellowship. What he found amazing about this course was that he realised after being sober for the first time in years, he had never stopped to question his actions and take responsibility for them. He had never had that clarity before. This was a turning point for Simon.

After being released from prison, Simon was cared for by Christians in various churches. He has married again and now works as part of the Prayer Ministry Team at a Christian healing and prayer centre.

Today it is hard to imagine Simon having lived a life of crime. He is now a very gentle and caring man who is fully committed and dedicated to his faith, family and church. The Bible tells us that God can work every situation for the good of those who love Him and He has certainly done this for Simon[17].

---

[17] Original story source: 'A Journey from Revenge to Restoration' blog on www.prisonfellowship.org.uk. Used by permission.

CHAPTER SIX

Sally's Story

Sally grew up in a Christian home. Her father was a Church of England warden and Sally went along to a nearby Methodist Sunday School every week.

This continued throughout her childhood. She went to church and tried to be a 'good' person. She would call herself a Christian, but there was no real relationship of any substance with Jesus. She knew God existed but did not know that He wanted a *relationship* with her.

Sally had now reached the age when it was time for her to go to Senior School. Time to leave the protective bubble of Primary School and begin to take those first few brave steps into a grown-up world. It was not long before Sally heard a boy swearing. She was shocked that the name of 'Jesus' was being used as a swear word and was terrified that this boy was going to be struck down by lightning.

Later while studying for her O-Level examinations, Sally chose to study Religious Education (RE) simply because her brother had also studied this a few years before her. At this time the course was completely Bible-based and the students were given a translation of the Bible that was easy to read and understand.

It was here where she began to meet God in a more real way. Her RE teacher was a born-again Christian. He encouraged them to write and make notes in their Bibles. He also made the subject come alive which was very different to a list of facts and a collection of stories that Sally had experienced in the past. The teacher allowed the pupils to ask questions that were off-syllabus and was happy to address issues that actually interested them.

Sally remembers one lesson in particular where they discussed the reasons people give for not becoming a Christian after they have heard the gospel message about Jesus dying for their sins. It was after this lesson that Sally decided to follow Jesus. But at this point it was her fear of going to Hell that helped her make the decision rather than a desire to fall in love with Jesus.

Within a day or two sinful habits had caught up with her and she had not managed to live this Christian life that she was trying so hard to live now. So she went to her RE teacher and told him what had happened. He explained that the whole point of living a Christian life is not about trying to do it on our own. In fact it is impossible to do so. You can't do it on your own because you need Jesus' power within you in order to do it. He has paid the price for all our sin and we need to invite Him into our lives and trust Him. We need to allow Him to work within us and He will help us to stay away from sin and live the kind of life that pleases Him.

Even after this, it took Sally many years to completely understand the gospel message. She found it difficult to accept that she did not need to earn her salvation by trying to be good, that it is a free gift that only needs accepting. Because of this, in the early days of her Christian walk Sally found it very difficult as she was continually striving for perfection in her own strength and never achieved it, so would be miserable.

About a year after becoming a Christian Sally became even more miserable because she made some choices that lead her away from God for a time. She found herself in a situation where she was longing to please God but was allowing sin to take hold of her.

At the age of twenty, Sally began to seek God again. This made her realise how much she needed His forgiveness and His grace. She now realised that there was no strength of her own that could keep her safe, away from sin. Now she wanted to be a Christian because she loved Jesus because of what He had done for her, because He gave so much in order for her to be set free. She was no longer afraid of going to Hell.

Since this time, Sally's relationship with Jesus has grown and developed. Her relationship with Him is her anchor in life. Jesus helps her to cope with the difficulties and challenges of life that come her way. She realises that this life is temporary but no matter what happens God is always with her and one day she will be with Him face to face. She is also grateful that she is part of a church family where she can meet with like-minded people. This is a lifeline for Sally as it is a place of love and acceptance where everyone is travelling the journey of faith together.

CHAPTER SEVEN

Terry's Story

At fourteen his parents divorced. At fifteen he received his first prison sentence. At sixteen he left school. He was living a life of violence and crime, full of anger and heavy drinking. This is how life began for Terry.

Violence came easy for him. At this time in his life with no job prospects, he set about trying to get a name for himself. This behaviour led to many court appearances and sentences. One area of violence he particularly enjoyed was at and around football matches. He was a young man, full of anger and devoid of hope, looking for the next piece of excitement in an otherwise tedious existence.

This destructive cycle continued for many years. Terry's various times in prison only served to make him angrier. As time went by he swapped his alcohol addiction for drugs. This led to problems at home. The drink and drugs put a big strain on his relationship with his partner. He did try to deal with his addiction problems but this did not really work and his behaviour became very erratic.

His mental health had also suffered and when the day came when his partner told him that their relationship was over and that he must leave the family home, he snapped.

He climbed up onto the roof of the family home. Terry was in a terrible state. He began throwing roof tiles down onto the crowd that was gathering below, making a hole through which to jump. At this point he wanted his life over with. His addictions had taken over and he couldn't beat them. His family no longer wanted anything to do with him. He was angry, depressed and desperate. He just wanted it all to end.

Within ten to fifteen minutes of climbing onto the roof the police arrived. A police negotiator was trying to talk him down. However, despite his best efforts, Terry decided to jump.

Terry was an atheist at the time but as he wrapped the coaxial cable from the TV aerial around his neck he said: "If there is a God, I'm coming to meet you". At that moment he was flooded with a sense of peace that words cannot describe. He just knew that he was going to be safe. In that moment he knew that God was real and that Jesus had saved him.

Then he jumped.

At this point he lost consciousness. He was rushed to hospital where he spent a week in intensive care fighting for his life.

In the months and years that followed this event, Terry met up with some of the emergency services workers who were there on that day. One of the paramedics told Terry that it was a miracle he had survived – he was expecting to bring out the body bag.

Sometime after his recovery, Terry now knew Jesus was real and so he felt he had to connect with him. So through a friend, he was invited to church. At this point he was very broken and not in a good place. But to his surprise he found the people in the church to be very welcoming and friendly. He felt this was where he needed to be.

And so the healing process began.

Several years later Terry is now very close with his family and has a good relationship with his ex-partner. God has used his past negative experience and has turned it round for the good, as he now works with the homeless and ex-offenders. Terry loves the serving aspect of his faith. He is now loving and open, which is the total opposite of how he was before he allowed God into his life to change him. He can relate to those who are broken and alone and can help others on the path to freedom.

People who knew Terry from the past often see him around the town and notice the change in him. They see first-hand the difference Jesus has made which Terry believes is more effective than him preaching at them.

Another massive change for Terry is that he now likes himself. He is content and at peace. This in turn helps him to love other people too. He has apologised to a lot of people for his past lifestyle but it is over now. He is determined not to live or dwell on the past, but to look ahead and keep moving forward to a brighter future.

He admits that there are still things he needs to work on, but he is more than happy to do so with God's help. He has met some wonderful people over the years and other Christians have had a big impact upon him. Terry feels he has now been given the tools to deal with life in the right way.

God has not only changed Terry's life, but every other life that touches his.

CHAPTER EIGHT

Verity's Story

Verity grew up in a Christian family. She has been going to church ever since she can remember. Her family prayed together and discussions about Jesus and faith were fairly common place around the home.

When she was a child, Verity remembers a few holidays where her family went along to a Christian holiday conference together called Spring Harvest. One of the strengths of this particular Bible week is that it caters for the whole family and she really enjoyed the children's programme that was on offer. Not only did she feel less isolated in a country where Christianity is not very popular she also had a lot of fun learning more about who Jesus really is.

She recalls one occasion when she was about eleven years old, she was at Spring Harvest and she really felt that she agreed with what the Bible teacher was saying in that children's meeting. It was there that she decided to follow Jesus for herself, not just because it was a thing her family did. She prayer a prayer and dedicated her life to following Jesus. After this she asked her parents how old she had to be in order to be baptised. They explained that you could be any age to be baptised, but they were a little hesitant as they weren't quite sure if the commitment was genuine. It was still early days.

Verity's teenage years tested her faith. She was thirteen when she first encountered doubts about her belief in Jesus and she started to question things. She also got very angry with God at the pain associated with womanhood as well as the unfairness and inequality between the sexes. She also began to ask 'Is God there or not?'

It was during this time when Verity was also consumed by fear. She constantly dwelt on her worries and it got to the point where she was fearful even to leave the house. This really stretched her faith to the limit. She realised that her faith had to become greater than the negative thoughts in her head. She had to rely on God and His strength. Her faith had left the dusty shelves of theory and become real. She literally needed her faith in Jesus to help her live her life, to carry her through each day.

Over time she learnt how to fight these fears with God's strength and power within her. Things began to improve. Gradually she experienced more and more peace.

It was after this dark time when she decided to be baptised. She realised that she couldn't have changed without a *real* God helping her.

Verity explains her relationship with Jesus as a very gradual change. She knows there is a God who has transformed her from whom she was and who she could have become. God has saved her from herself!

Now she walks with God daily, continually trusting in Him. She tries to draw close and to understand what the Bible says, although she admits to finding this challenging. Verity is more involved in the life of her local church and has led a Bible study group. She admits she still gets scared when big life events occur, but she is free from the grip of fear now. She can be at peace in every circumstance knowing that God is truly in control.

CHAPTER NINE

What's Your Story?

As you have read through the various real-life true stories of a wide variety of people in the previous chapters, you can see how God's salvation plan has been practically worked out in different ways for each person. Some are dramatic and powerful, demonstrating God's power and showing that His salvation plan is for all people no matter their background. God is not interested in where you have come from, but in where you are going. It does not matter who you were, but who you will become.

Other stories are less dramatic, yet still just as powerful. These show that even if your life has not taken dramatic twists and turns, even if you live a fairly ordinary life God's salvation plan is available to you also. Quite often people strive to live a 'good' life. They obey the law, they try not to be unkind, they have friends, they invest time in their families and they work hard. Surely their goodness, their good deeds mean that God will look favourably upon them? By being a good person they believe they do not need 'saving' – saving from what?

The thing is – salvation is a gift. We cannot earn it, no matter how hard we try[18]. And sin still exists! Jesus' death broke its power, but it is still around and Satan is doing everything he can to destroy lives even to this day[19]. We continue to live under the curse of sin and separation from God unless we choose to accept His rescue plan for us. Jesus is Freedom. He offers us freedom from sin and only through Jesus can we be reconnected to God.

> ' Jesus answered, 'I am the way and the truth and the life. No one comes to the Father except through me. If

---

[18] Romans 6:23, Ephesians 2:8-9
[19] 1 Peter 5:8

you really know me, you will know my Father as well.'

(John 14:6-7, NIV)

A Friend of God

It is only through faith in Jesus that we can restore our relationship with God. The Bible tells us that it is possible to overcome the separation from God caused by sin entering the world through Adam and Eve. This is because Jesus, the sinless one who has already paid the price for it by his death, takes our sin upon himself. God now sees us, sinless and unblemished because of Jesus' sacrifice on the cross.

So we can become friends of God. We can walk with Him and talk with Him. He longs to have a relationship with us, his precious creation. Humanity was created for relationship. There is no greater relationship than that of humanity with God.

'You are my friends if you do what I command. I no longer call you servants, because a servant does not know his master's business. Instead, I have called you friends, for everything that I learned from my Father I have made known to you.'

(John 15:14-15, NIV)

What is Salvation?

Salvation is a fancy word that acknowledges the fact that we accept we are in trouble; we are in a place in our life where we know we need to be rescued from the mess, the pain and sin we find ourselves in. We realise we need to be saved. As is the case in so many superhero movies, one of the characters finds themselves caught up in some serious trouble with no way out. At least, there seems to be no way out from their perspective. What is needed is someone from outside the situation to step in and scoop them up – to rescue, or save them. Most often this is where the superhero swoops in and saves the day. However, in this instance we recognise that the person who needs rescuing is us. We would be right to recognise that living under this curse of sin there is no way out. There is no escape through our own effort. What we need is someone outside of sin, someone stronger than death itself to step in and save us.

Salvation is a Decision

Salvation is a process. It is not a magic formula, but a relationship that grows and develops and looks different for each individual – as you can tell from the collection of stories earlier in the book. The Bible, which is God's love letter and instruction manual on how to live life His way, shows us certain stages of the process. Although each stage is important, how it works itself out in your life may be different from someone else's experience. For example certain stages may happen together at the same time, or some may be spread out over a year or so. Sometimes even the order of events may switch around a little. Jesus knows you and He knows your life. He also knows your heart and will be happy if you are doing what He is telling you to do, when He tells you to do it. It doesn't matter if it may look a little different from someone else's experience – you are writing your own story with Jesus after all.

It all begins with a decision. You need to decide whether you believe in Jesus, or not. You need to decide whether you are willing to accept his rescue plan for your life, or not. You need to decide to live your life from now onwards with Jesus in control of it, or not. It all starts with a decision – your decision.

Saying Sorry and Turning Away

It is also important to say sorry to God for the sin in your life and make a commitment to turn around and walk, or even run, in the opposite direction from it! This is called repentance.

> 'Now it's time to change your ways! Turn to face God so he can wipe away your sins, pour out showers of blessing to refresh you, and send you the Messiah he prepared for you, namely, Jesus.'
>
> (Acts 3:19-20, The Message)

Some people have found saying a prayer, asking Jesus to come and rescue them, a helpful way of making this decision. Unfortunately some have taken it too far and see saying a prayer such as this as *the* method of gaining salvation. This is not true. It is merely a helpful aid, not a magic formula. However, if you think saying a prayer will help you to invite Jesus to come and rescue you, I have written one on the next page that you could say.

Prayer

Oh Jesus, I recognise that I am a sinner and that I have been living my life apart from you.

I know there is nothing I can do that will rescue me from the mess and sin that I am in.

Please forgive me of my sin.

Jesus, I believe that you are God's rescue plan for the world.

I believe that you died and rose again.

I invite you to show me how to live life your way.

I give my life to you.

Come and be in charge and in control.

Jesus, come and make all things new!

Amen

Believe it and Say it

One of the early stages of the process is believing and saying. The Bible puts it like this:

> 'If you declare with your mouth, 'Jesus is Lord', and believe in your heart that God raised him from the dead, you will be saved.'
>
> (Romans 10:9, NIV)

This is often the stage that many Christians remember and will tell you was the moment they *became* a Christian. This part of the process, like the others, is beautifully simple yet extremely powerful.

There are many ways this can be done. Here are a few ideas:

Say aloud with your mouth 'Jesus is Lord' and believe in your heart that God raised him from the dead. You could even do it right now where you sit as you read this book? Speak it aloud and believe it.

Another way you could 'speak it' is by telling another person about your decision. This could be someone from your family, or better still, another Christian who can help you as you begin your own relationship with Jesus.

Again you may find saying the prayer on page 86e another helpful way of declaring with your mouth what your heart believes.

Being Baptised

Another stage along the journey of salvation is that of water baptism. Most Christian churches recognise baptism as being an important part of the salvation process. Although there is a lot of debate between them as to *how* it is done.

So what is water baptism? Water baptism is a symbolic act that a Christian takes part in as a public sign of their belief in Jesus. It involves the person being totally submerged underneath the water. A declaration of faith in Jesus is made by the person being baptised and prayers are said.

Full submersion imitates the baptism Jesus received by John the Baptist[20] in The Bible and the symbolism is powerful and poignant. As we die to our old pre-Jesus selves we are buried

---

[20] Matthew 3

underneath the water. Then we rise up again into a new life in Jesus, having our sins washed away both inside out[21]!

> 'Whoever believes and is baptised will be saved, but whoever does not believe will be condemned'
>
> (Mark 16:16)

> 'Repent and be baptised, every one of you, in the name of Jesus Christ for the forgiveness of sins. And you will receive the gift of the Holy Spirit.'
>
> (Acts 2:38)

One thing to point out is that it is never too late! If you have decided to live your life in a relationship with Jesus, you should be baptised.

---

[21] Romans 6:3-6

Receive the Holy Spirit

So who is the Holy Spirit and why should we receive him? Jesus told His followers that once He went up into heaven, after He had risen again, He would send a helper / friend:

> 'If you love me, show it by doing what I've told you. I will talk to the Father, and he'll provide you another Friend so that you will always have someone with you. This Friend is the Spirit of Truth.'
>
> (John 14:15-17, The Message)

Christians believe that God exists as three equal persons: God the Father, God the Son (Jesus) and God the Holy Spirit. These three together are one! They are different expressions of the same being. This is why Jesus is both fully human and fully God and why only He was able to break the curse of sin and death.

The Holy Spirit can be invited to live within us, to enliven our own spirit - to refresh and rejuvenate us from within. The Holy Spirit also helps us communicate with Jesus as He is in effect *Jesus' spirit*. When we talk with the Holy Spirit, we are also talking with Jesus. The Holy Spirit helps to bring understanding when we read the Bible. The Holy Spirit can give dreams or mental images. The

Holy Spirit lets us know what is right and what is wrong and also gives us a deep sense of sadness and regret when we have sinned – to lead us back to Jesus by saying sorry. When the Holy Spirit is at work in our lives we will begin to notice certain elements of our character begin to grow and develop. These are called 'fruits of the Spirit':

> 'But the fruit of the Spirit is love, joy, peace,
> forbearance, kindness, goodness,
> faithfulness, gentleness and self-control. Against such
> things there is no law.'
>
> (Galatians 5:22-23)

The Bible also speaks of certain gifts that the Holy Spirit can give to a person[22]. These gifts can help a person live a Christian life on an individual level and some are to help a collection of Christians function well as a group, or a church. Now not everyone will receive every gift[23], but the Bible does encourage us to ask for them.

The Holy Spirit brings the supernatural. The Holy Spirit allows the power of God to dwell inside us and to work through us – the

---

[22] 1 Corinthians 12:7-11
[23] 1 Corinthians 12:4-6

same power that raised Jesus from the dead! We are fighting against a supernatural enemy, Satan. We need supernatural power to fight him because we are completely unable to stand against him in our own strength. This is what the Holy Spirit brings us.

> 'And if the Spirit of him who raised Jesus from the dead is living in you, he who raised Christ from the dead will also give life to your mortal bodies because of[c] his Spirit who lives in you.'

(Romans 8:11)

So what does it mean to 'receive the Holy Spirit'? In a similar way to asking Jesus to come into your life and to forgive you of your sin, this is when you ask the Holy Spirit to come into your heart. It is basically issuing an open invitation to the Holy Spirit to live inside your spirit, to lead you and direct you. This is often done through prayer. You could simply pray right now and ask Jesus to fill you with His Holy Spirit. Some people find it useful to ask a fellow Christian to pray for or with them. Simply ask, then wait and receive. Sometimes strange supernatural things happen when the Holy Spirit enters a person, just like it did on the day of Pentecost when the Holy Spirit first entered Jesus' followers[24]. But

---

[24] Acts 2

sometimes nothing particularly strange or amazing happens. It is different for each person. Pray and receive the Holy Spirit by faith – believe you have received Him simply because you asked and Jesus wants to give you good things, especially the Holy Spirit. Know that when you ask, Jesus will respond:

> ' Which of you fathers, if your son asks for a fish, will give him a snake instead? Or if he asks for an egg, will give him a scorpion? If you then, though you are evil, know how to give good gifts to your children, how much more will your Father in heaven give the Holy Spirit to those who ask him!'
>
> (Luke 11:11-13)

The Road Less Travelled

If you have made the decision to ask Jesus in to your life – Congratulations! Welcome to the world-wide family of God. The first chapter of your story has now begun. By asking Jesus into your life your sins have been forgiven. Your relationship with God has been restored and your place living in an eternity with him is assured.

Just as any other relationship you have requires work, dedication and commitment, so does your relationship with Jesus. Things will take time, but will be well worth it. Take heart, believe and persevere.

Living a Christian life can be tough, challenging and even painful. Jesus does not promise us an easier life. Jesus does rescue us from our sin but unlike the superhero, He does not pull us out of the bad situation. Rather He gives us the strength to live through it and survive. He fights for us. He enables us. Yes, our sins are forgiven but there is still much to learn. Sometimes it is through the hard times that we learn to trust God more. Jesus will work on your character, changing you and transforming you into who God intended you to be before the curse of sin got hold of you. This transformation process can be painful, it can also be pleasant. Just as a potter forming a beautiful pot out of clay needs to pinch it and shape it, so too will God begin to shape your life.

Use Your Gym Membership

I have been a member of several gyms over the years. It starts out in a whirlwind of excitement and determination – I know exercise is good for me! I enthusiastically join a gym and attend regularly for about the first four weeks. After a while the excitement and euphoria starts to wear off and the hard work of my task begins to take over my focus. My use of the gym starts to reduce. Soon the weather changes and I don't want to go on the journey to get to the gym because it is too dark, or too wet, or I've just come back from a bad day at work. Eventually I stop going altogether. I still have the gym membership card in my wallet, but I'm not really a member of the gym because I don't go. On paper I'm a member, but in reality and in my heart, I am not.

Becoming a Christian can be compared to taking out a gym membership. It can be very exciting when we first encounter Jesus and start to learn things about him and about how our lives are supposed to be lived. However, we must guard against falling into the 'bad gym member' mentality – where we are only a member on paper, but in reality our behaviour and our heart says otherwise.

As you start out on your journey of faith in a wonderful and personal relationship with Jesus, here are a few suggestions from a fellow traveller that will hopefully be of some use.

If you haven't already done so, tell someone of your decision to follow Jesus, especially your close family. They may not agree with you, but hopefully they will support your decision.

Try to find other Christians to share your journey with. Growing together, worshipping together and walking the journey of faith together are vital in helping the fires of faith to keep burning brightly in your heart. This may be found in a life-giving church, or around someone's home.

Begin to read the Bible. The Bible is God's love letter to us. It is also God's instruction manual on how we are to live our lives His way, the right way, free from sin. I would suggest trying to find an easily understood translation such as the NIV (New International Version) or The Message. I would also suggest you begin by reading parts of the New Testament which you will find about two-thirds away from the beginning. If you want to start small, try reading some of the shorter letters that Paul wrote such as Ephesians or 1 & 2 Timothy. If you want to know more about salvation Romans is a good place to start. If you want to learn more about Jesus, then try Matthew, Mark, Luke or John. This will make a good start and will hopefully be more easily understood than some parts of the Old Testament. However, the Old Testament is extremely important so don't ignore it. Get started with the New Testament and when you feel ready, have a go at some parts of the Old Testament.

Have conversations with Jesus. Prayer is simply having a chat with Jesus. This can be done aloud or quietly within your heart. As in any relationship, good communication is a vital ingredient. Prayer is a two-way conversation between you and Jesus. Don't be surprised when you get a response or an answer to your prayer. It is unlikely to be a voice you can hear (although this can happen). Rather it could be a 'gut feeling'; a picture you can 'see' with your mind's eye; something happening in the world around you; a particular phrase from the Bible that you just *know* is for you and your situation. Again, prayer is something that takes time to learn. Have patience, but keep on practising. You will soon get into it and will find a way of praying that works for you.

Ask questions. I believe it is important that we all know why we believe what we believe. Being curious about some of the things the Bible says, or about some of the things you hear in church that you don't quite understand is a good thing. This is one advantage of having other Christians around you who have found answers to these questions for themselves over a period of time. Another place to look for answers is to read books about the subject. Again, speak to other Christians who will be able to recommend a few helpful titles to you. It will help you grow in your faith as well as in your knowledge of God.

Blessed Assurance

It is quite common for people who have recently asked Jesus into their hearts to begin to have doubts a few days later if what they have done has actually happened or is real. The enemy of our souls, Satan is out to get us[25] and wants nothing more than for you to reject the salvation that Jesus brings. Jesus breaks Satan's power[26] and rescues you from his grasp and he doesn't like it. So doubts will come but there is no need to be afraid. You can be certain of your salvation. Jesus himself gives us His assurance:

> ' I give them eternal life, and they shall never perish; no one will snatch them out of my hand. My Father who has given them to me, is greater than all; no one can snatch them out of my Father's hand.'
>
> (John 10:28-29)

---

[25] 1 Peter 5:8
[26] Romans 6:6-8

'For God so loved the world that he gave his one and only Son, that whoever believes in him shall not perish but have eternal life'

(John 3:16)

You've Only Just Begun

So perhaps your story with Jesus has just begun. I would love to read your 'chapter' of this book – the story of how *you* came to know Jesus. You can share it with me by emailing me on my website www.mattmcchlery.com if you like.

Thank you for allowing me to play a small part in your story. Life is an adventure and living it with Jesus makes the ride all the more enjoyable. I hope that as the days turn into months, and the months turn into years, and as you become a seasoned traveller along the journey of faith, you will be able to see how God has made all things new for you too.

Thanks

Firstly, thank you to Jesus for saving me! Without Him there would be no reason to write this book or to sing the songs.

Thank you to The King's Church, Wisbech family who have continued to walk with me and 'do' life together over the past decade or so. Thank you too for being a church community who are open and accepting of people no matter their background. Indeed the stories contained within these pages have all come from the lives of people from within our church. In particular thank you to Fiona, Sally, Bob, Simon, Terry and Verity for sharing your stories.

Thanks to Clive Butcher for checking the theological accuracy; Gareth Lowe for pointing me in the right direction in the final chapter; Patrick Johnstone for all your help and advice as to how a book fits together as well as suggestions of things I hadn't even thought of including. Anna Smith and Pauline Stevens for proofreading. Thanks also to those who gave of their time in their busy schedules to read and endorse this book: Cris Rogers, Tony Cummings, Gareth Lowe and Rob McFarlane, it is much appreciated.

Thank you to my wife and family for your continued support throughout the years. For keeping me focused on getting this book finished. For giving me the space and time in order to do it as well as reminding me when family takes priority. I love you all very dearly.

Thank you to the doctors and medical professionals who have helped and supported me so well over the past year and for all you will do in the years to come.

Finally, thanks to you, dear reader, for picking up this book and reading it through to the end. I pray that it will have encouraged and blessed you and maybe even helped you to start to write your own story with Jesus.

About The Author

Matt McChlery is a singer, songwriter, worship leader, author, blogger and primary school teacher. His songs have been sung in churches around the world and his blog has been a Finalist in the national Premier Digital Awards twice and has received over 100 000 views. His song 'Fingerprints' achieved Finalist position in the UK Songwriting Competition. Diagnosed with cancer in 2016, Matt's passion is to make every moment count for God's Kingdom! Originally from Zimbabwe, Matt now lives with his wife, Verity and their three children in the United Kingdom.

Books
by Matt McChlery

Songcraft: Exploring the Art of Christian Songwriting

All Things New: Stories of Transformed Lives

Albums & EPs
by Matt McChlery

Fly

A Deeper Longing

All Things New

No One Like Jesus

The Amazing 6-Track CD that Accompanies this Book: 'All Things New'

'There is so much quality that oozes out of these songs'.

- Louder Than The Music

Available as digital download from all good digital music retailers.

CDs available from **www.mattmcchlery.com**

Matt McChlery's Debut Full-Length Worship Album: 'FLY'

'Matt's songs are up there with the best of them'
- Cross Rhythms

Available as digital download from all good digital music retailers.

CDs available from **www.mattmcchlery.com**

Acoustic Worship 5-Track CD:

'A Deeper Longing'

'Tried and tested congregational songs work well in this stripped down setting' - Cross Rhythms

Available as digital download from all good digital music retailers.

CDs available from **www.mattmcchlery.com**

A book packed full of tips and techniques for the Christian Songwriter: 'Songcraft'

'Whether you're a novice or have been crafting songs for years, this book will really empower you in your gift"
– Loulita Gill (Singer /Songwriter)

Available as digital download from all good digital book retailers.

Paperbacks available from **www.mattmcchlery.com**

Printed in Great Britain
by Amazon

22251966R00059